Trans-Generational Trauma

Thomas Hodge

Table of Contents

Trans-generational Trauma

Ecological factors have deep impact upon the development of an individual by clearly influencing understanding through long lasting modifications to an individual's understanding of the world in way that is incredibly difficult to change. A primary ecological concept that can be seen as clearly affecting the thinking of people is trans-generational trauma. Trans-generational trauma works on a premise much like trans-generational poverty. The concept of inter-generational poverty can be used to set the ground work for an understanding into how trans-generational trauma works.

In the poverty concept, poverty cycles through families due to the transference of behaviors from parent to child that can be seen as behaviors that are more associated with living in poverty and providing children with tools that would inhibit their ability to escape. Younger generations would lack the tools necessary to change their socio-economic standing. The tools that are of particular interest in studies of trans-generational poverty are the understanding of how ideas and generalizations are presented to younger generations, and the younger generations will build upon the ideas through a variety processes which have been clearly studied and defined in psychological research.

In the occurrence of trans-generational trauma, one would ask what is kind of trauma can be transferred, and how is it transferred? In examining the issue, any kind of trauma could be transferred to proceeding generations. This could include experiences of oppression, slavery, Jim Crowe laws, ethnic cleansing, genocide, the Holocaust, impacts of being on both sides of racism, and many other experiences. Trans-generational trauma serves to answer numerous questions concerning why poor people fear condemnation from authority figures, why wars continue in the countries of the Middle East, why western cultures were so quick to accept Islamic fundamentalist as terrorists as opposed to terrorist of a western origin, and various other ethnographic issues. The potential understanding that this concept allows for provides a clear understanding of how we develop these stigmas and generalizations in some people but not others. With a better understanding of the transmission of the ideas that set the foundations for behaviors that inhibit growth and improvement, one can set in motion necessary action needed to produce change throughout the society as a whole at least in sense of future generations.

For this concept to be a sound theory, the basis for how the transmission occurs must be established. Research has looked at the concept from a few different angles and viewpoints. Volkan (2001) explained the concept through group identity theory in that generations associated with the group identity, and past trauma is seen as a threat to that person's identity. Srour and Srour (2006) examined the issue through a case study in which they found it to be tied to emotional motivations as a response to communal stress.

Wohl and Van Bavel (2011) found that PTSD symptoms and behaviors were more prevalent in descendants of Holocaust survivors as opposed similar Jewish individuals that were not descendants of Holocaust survivors. In light of such research, one could imagine that trauma cycles through families from one generation to the next. Things are not so simple in reality because the proceeding generations never experienced the trauma, but there is an effect upon the future generations that can be seen to be connected to the trauma of the past.

This type of transference can be easily explained when one considers how an individual learns. In trans-generational trauma, younger generations are learning behaviors that are associated with the trauma from the older generations. This can be seen as inadvertently teaching younger generations to behave in an abnormal manner that is ungrounded in events directly related to the young generation's life experiences. Trans-generational trauma allows for the symptoms of a mental illness or condition to be transferable through learning to future generations. In these cases, people really do what they know, and the younger generations only know how to act in a manner that is similar to a traumatized individual. This is because their family acts this way. Since poor families tend to live in a more communal environment, the mesosphere and exosphere levels of the individual's ecological make-up re-enforce the behaviors exhibited by the parents because they would have experienced similar trauma or would have learned the trauma behavior in a similar indirect manner from social interactions with other traumatized or trans-generationally traumatized individuals.

Transfer of the behaviors occurs in simple manner at first and then is reinforced and magnified over time. The behaviors are first learned through social learning as explained by Bandura (1977) as the learning of knowledge through observation. Children observe the implicit behaviors of the parents. The children attempt to rationalize the behaviors and associate the behaviors with emotions that drive such behaviors. If an adult becomes tense around the police, the child will learn to become tense. Piaget (1950) explains that there are two types of ways in which individuals learn information. Early in development, the child learns by assimilation. During that time, new information is associated with per-existing schema and ideas. Later the child learns by accommodation in which the child develops new categories of schemata and is able to modify and adjust older schemata. However, the initial schemata can be reinforced over time and become more difficult to change.

Several generalizations are produced over time throughout development that lead to the reinforcement of the behaviors, cognitions, and emotions associated with traumatic events. In the example of the child learning to become tense in relation to an authority figure, the child will later become tense as a physiological response to other stimuli and events. The child will associate the tenseness with both all situations. The child may not fully understand why the parent is tense in association to authority figures, but the child will understand that one becomes tense as response to a fight or flight situation. In connecting the two categories, the child will associate authority figures such as the police and doctors as being threats that they must either oppose with a fight response or escape through use of a flight response. Similar patterns of development exist in other instances of trans-generational trauma.

The pattern is set forth through this theory showing how behaviors progress over time and generations in response to events that happened many generations back. As the child grows, the behaviors are reinforced through repeated instances of being exposed to similar situations. Once the child enters the social world of the education system, these behaviors have been engrained in the child's thought process. The response to the trauma of past generations has become normal to the child without their full understanding of why because the child knows no different. The child's thought pattern is the only way they know how to think. There should be no reason for them to see it as abnormal because they have developed with that pattern of thinking. Typically, the community, teachers, and various other important figures in the child's life think along the same lines of thought as the child's family because they are all interconnected through the levels of ecology. No one realizes anything should be different. It is just the way things are.

Change occurs as a few individuals in the society come to realize that the pattern of thought is not normal and they wander about what the grounds are which cause individuals to think along that line of thought. Frustrations set in as there is a conflict between change and stagnation. For the trauma to be removed, the entire ecological system would need to change and adjust. To change an individual's schemata after the schemata have been reinforced through such a high degree of repetition would be extremely difficult. The key to change is to attempt to modify the schemata as early as possible through early childhood education. In doing so, the issue of cultural preservation must be addressed. This early childhood education would need to serve as attempt not to destroy an ethnic group's culture. It would serve to unravel some of the trauma that has been embedded in that culture. To have cultural identity is seen as serving to preserve the history of a people. Cultural identity should, however, serve as a positive associate for people to connect without having a negative impact on the functioning of an individual through behaviors associated with traumatic events of past generations. If positive change is to be created, individuals will need to change adjust the flow of trans-generational behaviors from one generation to the next for the purpose of inhibiting emotions that were born of trauma while understanding and remembering why the cycle is to be broken.

Review of the Research

With regards to presenting the various research on the topic of trans-generational, one can notice a myriad of differing viewpoints on the factors that contribute to the phenomenon. To illustrate this appropriately, each of the research materials should be examined independently of one another first. Several of the approaches can be synthesized into collaborative models that interconnect and dynamically interact with each other. In this case, it is best to examine the current research independently. One can then make appropriate decisions on which approaches are acceptable as being an accurate depictions and explanations of the conditions and which approaches should be rejected.

Inter-generational trauma through terror

Kaitz, M., Levy, M., Ebstein, R., Faraone, S. V., & Mankuta, D. (2009).
The inter-generational effects of trauma from terror: A real
possibility. *Infant Mental Health Journal, 30*(2), 158-179.

Kaitz et al. (2009) examined the effect of inter-generational trauma through terror (ITTT). The researchers provided several examples of how severe trauma effects children through the mannerisms of the parents. Kaitz et al. (2009) found that anxiety and depression that resulted from the trauma produced discord that manifested in the responses of the parent to the child, mistimed and lack of appraisal, and criticism control on the part of the parent. Since the parent would have pronounced difficulty maintaining their own emotional responses, social interactions between the parent and child would have been marked by hindrances to adequate interactions as would be typically expected in most parent-child dyads. As the relationship was affected by the trauma, the attachment between parent and child became very insecure due to the inadequate responses from the parent toward the child's needs, fears, and frustrations.

The authors proposed that the trauma would affect not only the relationship between parent and child but also biologically impact the child. The mothers who experienced PTSD symptoms during pregnancy had significantly lower levels of cortisol. The lower levels of cortisol are often associated with anxiety disorders and have an impact on the HPA-axis. While in prenatal stages of development, the child is provided with significantly lower than usually levels of cortisol that produces an impact on the infant's regulation of the HPA-axis. The HPA-axis plays a key role in metabolism, memory, and immunity. When cortisol levels are too high or low, the HPA-axis is affected by the imbalance of the cortisol. As the authors mention such a biological impact, they emphasis the impacts of ITTT through both biological and environmental factors.

Nostalgia

Frankish, T., & Bradbury, J. (2012). Telling stories for the next

    generation: Trauma and nostalgia. Peace And

    Conflict: *Journal Of Peace Psychology, 18*(3), 294-306.

    doi:10.1037/a0029070

Frankish and Bradbury (2012) examined the inter-generational transmission of trauma as a result of apartheid in South Africa. Through their research, the researchers found that silence about the trauma between family members and nostalgia contributed to the effects of the trauma. Nostalgia served to define to the younger generations how life was so drastically changed by the events of the apartheid. Grandparents tell stories to grandchildren about how much better life was before the traumatic event and reflect that things were never the same after. Since all the children know is what life is like after the trauma, they assume a role of individuals that were directly affected by the traumatic events even though they never personally experienced the events.

Frankish and Bradbury (2012) noted that younger generations responded to the older generations when discussing the trauma of the apartheid as if they experienced the events themselves also. The best example was given when one of the children of an apartheid survivor answered questions about the survivor asked about events that occurred during apartheid, which happened before the younger individual was born. The traumatic events were discussed among family members rarely. The scarcity of the stories of trauma enriches the stories with a sense of novelty. The elders mentioned the stories only a few times to the younger generation so that the silence between the times that it is discussed strengthens the traumatic events and provides a connection for the younger generation to the events. The younger generation is often referred to as a "hinge" generation that is not yet free from the effects of the trauma but still a step toward making the trauma a notable history of their culture.

The article serves to show how storytelling between generations serves to provide a tie between the recent generations and the current generation so that the scars of a specific trauma carry on through history. This shows how that inter-generational transmission serves to display how severe a traumatic occurrence is based upon how relevant the experience feels for proceeding generations. The effect of the trauma can be seen also by the way that younger generations also see the trauma as separating them from the nostalgia of the past that is magnified by silence.

Storytelling

Baranowsky, A. B., Young, M., Johnson-Douglas, S., Williams-Keeler,

L., & McCarrey, M. (1998). PTSD transmission: A review of

secondary traumatization in Holocaust survivor

families. *Canadian Psychology, 39*(4), 247-256.

doi:10.1037/h0086816

Baranowsky et al. (1998) explored how the children
of holocaust survivors presented PTSD-like symptoms even
though they had never experienced trauma. In the research,
the children were found to be hyper-vigilant and untrusting
of others. The children also report that they felt different
from their peers and realized that they acted differently
also. The research did address that the populations that
were looked at were clinical populations that had came to
the attention of mental health professionals by self-referral.
Additionally, due to the nature of the holocaust, random
sampling would be impossibility preventing a true

experiment.

Baranowsky et al. (1998) addresses a variety of theories that has been used to explain the appearance of the symptoms in subsequent generations. The secondary PTSD could be explained as a symptom of deep understanding of the following generation about the prior generation in an attempt to understand their parents' struggles during the World War II era. The symptoms were also explored as being the product of storytelling compounded by silent periods. An evolutionary approach to the behaviors poses that the symptoms serve to be the younger generations reaction to the parents' attempts at teaching their children how to survive in times of persecution. This could be seen as an explanation based the concept of individuals' attempting to aid their genes in being based on through time. To promote the chances of lineage continuation, the survivors of the older generation develop attachment-styles and behave in ways that aide their children's survival based on the experiences of their lives when they were younger.

The author proposes that the transmission of trauma between generations could serve to set the expectations of clinicians treating PTSD sufferers. In light of such research, one should also look for symptoms of inter-generational transmission in the children of clients suffering from PTSD. The research does not provide a likelihood of transmission due to the claimed impossibility of designing such an experiment.

Parenting Style

Field, N. P., Om, C., Kim, T., & Vorn, S. (2011). Parental styles in

second generation effects of genocide stemming from the

Khmer Rouge regime in Cambodia. *Attachment & Human

Development, 13*(6), 611-628.

doi:10.1080/14616734.2011.609015

Field et al. (2011) examined the effects of trauma

due to trauma experienced during the Khmer Rouge

genocide in Cambodia upon the parenting styles of

survivors and the effects upon the proceeding generation.

The researchers examined how attachment styles correlated

with the trauma experienced by the parents and the anxiety

and depression symptoms that were displayed in the

children. The researchers found that the parents displayed a

role reversal in the style of attachment. Typically, a child

will look to a parent for emotional support. In the case of

the Khmer Rouge survivors, the trauma of the parents

reversed this interaction to where the parents began to look to the children as a source of emotional support in dealing with the parents' own past trauma.

The parents' traumatic experience served to provide a direct correlation with the children's levels of anxiety. The increased levels of anxiety could be seen as the result of the children having to cope with not only the stresses of growing up but also the stresses that resulted from being looked to for emotional support by the parent who was coping with PTSD from past events. The research also found a correlation between the trauma symptoms and the over-protectiveness of the maternal parent. The correlations of trauma to both role reversal and over-protectiveness serve to show two changes to parenting styles that are connected to traumatic experiences. Over-protectiveness and role reversals serve as the vehicle of transmission in the cases of anxiety and depression symptoms being transferred across generations as the result of events that were experienced by the parent.

Field et al. (2011) serves to be a comparison of the effects of trauma across cultures. Many psychological phenomena do not carry their effects from one culture to another. In the case of inter-generational trauma, the effects seem to be pronounced in not only the Jewish survivors of the Holocaust but also in the Asian survivors of the Khmer Rouge regime. This finding can be seen as the effect being shown across cultures or as trauma survivors existing as a separate culture unto themselves due to the differences in parenting styles and norms of thought that can be seen as uniquely different between those who have survived such significant large-scale trauma and those of the same culture who have not or have not descended from a survivors.

Alcohol Abuse

Myhra, L. L. (2011). It runs in the family: Inter-generational

transmission of historical trauma among urban American

Indians and Alaska Natives in culturally specific sobriety

maintenance programs. *American Indian & Alaska Native

Mental Health Research: The Journal of the National Center,

18*(2), 17-40.

Myhra (2011) examined the effects of trauma upon
Native Americans across generations. The trauma that was
experienced by Native Americans through forced
assimilation and relocation during the nineteenth century
correlated to increased levels of alcohol abuse and alcohol
dependence. PTSD and substance abuse problems are often
co-morbid. The research found that individuals would turn
to substance abuse as a maladaptive coping strategy in
dealing with the anxiety and depression that resulted from
generations of oppression and racism. The racism and

oppression served as the traumatic events for past generations. The trauma that past generations experienced was then perpetuated as following generations experienced similar trauma that compounded the effects of the inter-generational transmission. This can be seen as a double trauma for the younger generations.

The article contains a few weaknesses that the author is aware. Primarily, the sample size is small with only thirteen participants. Additionally, there is not a true control group to be able to the findings. The research is more of an ethnographic case study that explores the effects of prior trauma upon the different generations. The research does allow a more personal look into the individual lives of people that have experienced inter-generational trauma. The research also provides a look at how the trauma affects the individuals during childhood, adolescence, and adulthood through a narrative interview.

The Libby Study

Gaensbauer, T. J. (2003). Inter-generational transmission of trauma:

The infant's experience. *Infant Mental Health Journal, 24*(5),

524-526. doi:10.1002/imhj.10080

Gaensbauer (2003) provides a detailed analysis of Libby who is an infant whose mother suffers from PTSD. The author provides an in-depth look at the connections between the mother's symptoms and Libby's behavior. The author provides three ways that Libby's behavior is affected by the PTSD symptoms. First, he addressed the stress that Libby would be exposed to as a result of the mother having difficulties managing their lives and witnessing the mother's distress caused by her symptoms. Second, her mother defined Libby's definition of fear. Since Libby had not developed a reference of what is considered dangerous in the world, she developed an understanding of what to fear by observing her mother's reactions to the environment, which were abnormal and maladaptive responses. The third manner that Libby was affected by her mother's psychopathology was the result her mother's inconsistent affect regulation and distorted perceptions of reality during interactions between the mother and daughter. The interactions would be pleasant at times, and other times, the interactions seem hostile and anxiety provoking to Libby. The irregularity in mother-daughter bonding could be seen as produce instability in Libby's attachment to her mother that would exacerbate her anxiety and distress.

Gaensbaur (2003) provides detail into the interactions between parent and child in the case of Libby who can be seen as experience inter-generational transmission of trauma. By looking into a single case, the author is able to draw attention to particular facets of the dynamic between the mother and daughter. The details of the particular case can then be compared to other cases of inter-generational trauma to consider possible trends that may have been overlooked in large sample size experiment. The weakness of the article is the possible subjectivity in the author's analysis. The subjectivity is made up for by providing some examples to explain his reasoning. This would allow a critique of the article to provide alternative explanations for the child's behaviors and manifestations of PTSD-like symptoms.

Protectiveness

Rowland-Klein, D., & Dunlop, R. (1998). The transmission of trauma across generations: identification with parental trauma in children of Holocaust survivors. *Australian & New Zealand Journal of Psychiatry, 32*(3), 358-369.

Rowland-Klein and Dunlop (1998) interviewed six individuals who were children of Holocaust survivors to determine what themes were present across the individuals that would have contributed to transmission of trauma across generations. The research revealed a number of themes that were consistent across the sample. First, the sample displayed a number of themes revolving around their parents' style of parenting. This theme could be seen in the comparison of their parents to other parents, concerns about over-protection, and issues with separation. The children also heavily identified with their parent's experiences in a subjective understanding of what the concentration camp experience was like for their parents. An additional finding in the study was that the second generation had showed a heightened state of awareness about the parents' status as being Holocaust survivors through both overt and covert understandings of their parents' story of survival. As a result of these factors, a message of mistrust and fear were transmitted to the second generation through messages about a need to survive in dangerous situations.

The researchers utilized an interview format to conduct the study with a small sample size that consisted of only females, which was a weakness of the study. Despite the weaknesses of the study, the article did present a detailed look at the individual cases and the emerging themes that appeared across the individuals. Additionally, the sample was a non-clinical sample, which serves to be unique because the individuals reported several pathological symptoms associated with PTSD such as hyper-vigilance, mistrust, nightmares, and persistent fears.

The article also served to divide the methods of transmission into two categories that include conscious and unconscious transmissions of trauma. In making this distinction between the methods of transmission, Rowland-Klein and Dunlop (1998) present the behaviors of the parents as being a dynamic interaction between the types of forces that magnifies the effect of transmission of trauma across generations.

Grandchildren

Iliceto, P., Candilera, G., Funaro, D., Pompili, M., Kaplan, K., &
Markus-Kaplan, M. (2011). Hopelessness, Temperament,
Anger and Interpersonal Relationships in Holocaust (Shoah)
Survivors' Grandchildren. Journal Of Religion & Health,
50(2), 321-329. doi:10.1007/s10943-009-9301-7

Illiceto et al. (2011) compared the differences
between the grandchildren of Holocaust survivors to that of
a control group that did not have grandparents who
experienced such trauma. The research found that the
differences could be found in how the individuals perceived
themselves and how they perceived others. The
grandchildren of survivors perceived others as being more
hostile and rejecting than the control group perceived
others to be. They also perceived both themselves and
others to be more submissive than the control group. The
inter-generational transmission had a deeper impact on the

way in which the grandchildren perceived others than themselves. In affecting their perception of others, the trauma influenced the individual's reactions to others. This type of perception of others can be seen to explain the grandchildren's mistrust and hyper vigilance to potential dangers that could be perceived as coming from other individuals.

The research did not explore the parenting or attachment styles that the individuals experienced as young children or adolescences. This is a shortcoming of the article. If the article were to examine the differences in parenting style to the behaviors presented by the children, the author would have been able to demonstrate how the behaviors were transmitted from parent to child as a result of the trauma. Without examining the potential differences of experiences with-in the groups, the author leaves an opening for the potential of a third variable to explain the differences between the experimental and control group. The article serves to show a correlation between particular outcomes in grandchildren and trauma experienced or not experienced by grandparents. The correlation also contains a weakness as the trauma experienced by the grandparents is only viewed as a dichotomous property as opposed to a continuous property based on the severity of the trauma experienced by the grandparents.

Father and child

Mellor, ,. J., Davidson, ,. C., & Mellor, D. J. (2001). The adjustment of

children of Australian Vietnam veterans: is there evidence for

the trans-generational transmission of the effects of war-

related trauma?.*Australian & New Zealand Journal Of

Psychiatry, 35*(3), 345-351. doi:10.1046/j.1440-

1614.2001.00897.x

Mellor, Davidson, and Mellor (2001) examined the differences between children of veteran fathers with PTSD, veteran fathers without PTSD, and civilian fathers. They found that the children of veteran fathers with PTSD displayed higher rates of PTSD symptomology. The two groups whose fathers did not have PTSD showed no difference from each other. In addition, the PTSD group showed lower levels of self-esteem, problem solving, and affective responsiveness. The symptoms of the original PTSD experienced by the father can be seen as having an impact on the attachment between the father and child, which would lead to maladaptive responses to interpersonal interaction. Frustrations that would be experienced when the child would attempt to overcome deficits in affection during a young age could explain the difficulty in problem solving among the children.

The research was well designed by having two groups to compare with the PTSD group. The two control groups serve to answer the possibility of differences between children growing up in a military family and those in a civilian family. The research also explores two facets of inter-generational trauma that has been ignored by many other research articles. First, the article explores the transmission of trauma between the father and the child. Other research has explored the connection between the mother and child but has ignored the possible transmission of trauma by way of the father. The research demonstrates that trauma is also likely to be transmitted from the father to the child also. In addition, the article explores the transmission of wartime trauma that was experienced by an individual who played a role of military personnel who is less of a direct and definable victim than civilians who had been traumatized during wartime events and clearly defined as victims of trauma. In exploring the connection between the father's trauma and the child's manifestation of PTSD like symptoms, the authors make a connection between the child's expression of PTSD and the parent's perceptions as opposed to third party perceptions and expectations.

Connections

Sagi-Schwartz, A. (2003). Introduction to the special issue: Extreme life events and catastrophic experiences and the development of attachment across the life span. *Attachment & Human Development, 5*(4), 327-329. doi:10.1080/14616730310001633465

Sagi-Schwartz (2003) explored the effect of trauma upon the parenting ability of the parent in cases of inter-generational trauma. The article posits that mothers who had experienced traumatic events such as the Holocaust, the genocide in Kosovo, rape, or the loss of a loved one lose confidence in their ability to be a safe base for attachment styles that encourage exploration. The author proposes that the trauma decreases the mother's self-esteem and confidence in her parental abilities because of how she was unable to protect herself from such harm. As a result, the child experiences an inadequate relationship with the parent to promote exploration and self-confidence. One can clearly note that the behaviors displayed by the parent are the results of the symptoms of PTSD that are then transmitted to the child. The child then recapitulates the behaviors that are observed and engaged by the parent as being appropriate and normal. This leads to the reactions to trauma being transferred from the parent to the child with the child responding to stimuli in a similar manner as the parent would respond based on the bias created by the traumatic experience.

The article serves to show how the connections between the traumatic event and the child's behavior or perceptions are connected. Sagi-Schwartz (2003) accomplishes this by comparing and contrasting the connections between other research articles and experiments. The article leaves fails to perform a statistical meta-analysis of the associated and supporting work. In doing so, this serves to be a major weakness of the article.

The organization of the connections between previous research serves to be a strong point of the article and provides the possibility for continued research into the connections made by the author.

7820398R00030

Printed in Great Britain
by Amazon.co.uk, Ltd.,
Marston Gate.